ESSENTIAL LIFE SKILLS

DEVELOPING

FINANCIAL LITERACY

by Samantha S. Bell

BrightPoint Press

San Diego, CA

BrightPoint Press

an imprint of ReferencePoint Press, Inc.
Printed in the United States

For more information, contact:
BrightPoint Press
PO Box 27779
San Diego, CA 92198
www.BrightPointPress.com

LIBRARY OF CONGRESS CATALOGING-IN-PUBLICATION DATA

Name: Bell, Samantha S., author.
Title: Developing financial literacy / by Samantha S. Bell.
Description: San Diego, CA: ReferencePoint Press, 2027 | Series: Essential life skills | Includes bibliographical references and index. | Audience: Grades 7–9
Identifiers: ISBN 9781678214524 (hardcover) | ISBN 9781678214531 (eBook)
The complete Library of Congress record is available at www.loc.gov.

CONTENTS

AT A GLANCE

- Teens can earn money in several ways. Many teens work in jobs such as babysitting or lifeguarding. Others wash cars and mow lawns, work in restaurants, or sell creative products.

- Jobs pay employees their earned salary through paychecks or direct deposit.

- People often keep their money in banks or credit unions.

- Budgeting helps people manage their money.

- A person's budget should take into account their goals, income, necessary spending, discretionary spending, and saving.

- Credit cards can help people borrow money and build credit.
- Saving and investing are key parts of building wealth. Building wealth helps people prepare for their future.
- Starting to invest early leads to the best results. The money can grow over time.

PAYDAY

Layla tied the apron strings around her waist. She slipped on her visor and pinned her nametag in place. She was finishing her first week at the Burger Barn.

When Layla walked out to the driveway, her mom was already in the car. Layla slipped into the passenger seat and buckled up. "It's payday!" Layla told her mom, smiling.

"You get paid every week?" Mom asked.

Some jobs, including food service jobs, require employees to wear certain clothing, such as aprons.

Older friends or family members may be a good source for advice about money.

"Yes! And I'm glad. I've heard that some jobs pay every 2 weeks," said Layla.

"And some jobs only pay once a month," Mom said. "You know, we can go by the bank after work today. You can set up a checking account. After that, the

Burger Barn can send your pay directly to your account. Getting paid that way is called direct **deposit**."

"They gave me a form to fill out about that," Layla said. "I have it in my bag."

"Let's take it with us to the bank," Mom said. "Have you thought about what you'll do with your money?"

"Grace is going to help me figure it out," Layla answered. Grace was Layla's older sister. She was home from college. "Grace said she'd help me set up a budget tonight. Whatever that is."

"A budget is a plan for how you will use your money," Mom said. "You can decide how much to use now on things you need. You can also decide how much to save for later."

Layla thought about the birthday money in her drawer. She remembered the babysitting cash she'd been saving. "Like saving up for those purple shoes I've been wanting?" she asked.

"Exactly. And for bigger goals, too," Mom said. "Like maybe saving up for college."

Layla's eyes lit up. "Or a car! I can look online for used cars. And by next summer, maybe I'll be ready to start driving myself to violin lessons," Layla said.

"Why not?" Mom agreed, smiling. She squeezed Layla's hand. "I'm so proud of you."

Layla grinned back at her mom. She couldn't wait to see what she could accomplish this summer.

Purchasing a used car is an achievable goal for many teens.

LEARNING FROM EARNING

Many teens look forward to earning their own money. But having a job has many other advantages, too. Jobs can help teens feel more independent. Teens can learn how to communicate with others. They also gain experience keeping commitments.

Parents and guardians often want their teens to learn financial literacy.

Even low-paying jobs teach valuable life skills. Rachel Greszler researches the economy. She says, "Low-wage, entry-level jobs provide the perfect opportunity for young people to learn the importance of key skills: showing up on time, getting along with co-workers, . . . and staying on task."[1] These things help teach financial literacy. That means knowing how to handle money wisely.

CHAPTER ONE

EARNING MONEY

Teens can earn **income** in several ways. Many young people babysit for friends and neighbors. They learn to solve problems and manage routines. Teens also earn money doing other odd jobs. These include moving furniture, washing cars, mowing lawns, or taking care of pets. Many of these jobs can be done throughout the year.

People may learn about jobs in their community from people they know, online posts, or community bulletin boards.

Many teens get their first jobs in the summer. They may be lifeguards or camp counselors. Fast food restaurants, cafés, grocery stores, and retail shops may hire teens, too. These places offer organized work environments and regular paychecks. Teens learn skills such as teamwork and accountability. Teens may work at these jobs during the school year, too.

Teens may also create their own jobs based on their interests. For example, some teens are skilled with social media. They may get jobs posting online content for small businesses. Teens who enjoy sports, music, or art can teach younger children. And teens who enjoy gardening, baking, or crafting can sell their products.

Some teens sell their products at farmers markets and craft fairs.

GETTING PAID

People get paid for their work in different ways. Teens who do odd jobs may receive cash or personal checks for their work. Stores, restaurants, or other businesses may give their employees paychecks. Those are checks made out to the employee from the business. Many people get paid electronically by direct deposit.

The money goes directly into the workers' bank accounts.

People often receive paystubs when they are paid. Paystubs can be physical or digital. Each paystub shows the gross pay, or total amount earned. However, this amount is not the amount that an employee gets to take home. Some money is taken

Many people use banking apps to keep track of money in their bank accounts.

out for taxes. Money may be taken out for **benefits**, too. So a paystub also lists the net pay. This is the money that the workers keep.

BANK IT

Banks are a key part of how most people manage their money. Banks are businesses. People deposit money into banks. For example, they may deposit money from their paychecks. The money is stored for them in accounts. Some are checking accounts. People can easily move money in and out. Others are savings accounts. These help people save up funds.

People can also get loans from banks. A bank gives someone a large sum of money. The person pays it back with a monthly payment. The payment includes extra fees. That way, the banks make money.

Most banks let teens open their own accounts once they reach a certain age. For younger teens, a parent or guardian can make a custodial account. This type of acount lets teens save and manage money with adult supervision.

Credit Unions

Credit unions are similar to banks. They also accept deposits and make loans. However, they are not owned by individuals. Members of the credit union have part of the ownership. In addition, credit unions are not businesses. When profits are made, the members gain sometihng. They may get lowered fees or extra money in their savings accounts.

Many banking tasks can be done online. However, banks often have physical locations as well.

Banks all have their own rules. For example, their accounts may have different rates or age restrictions. Teens should compare the rules before opening an account. Sophia Acevedo is a banking editor at the website Business Insider. She suggests, "I would look for a checking account that either doesn't have any monthly **service fees** or offers multiple ways to waive the fee."[2]

CHAPTER TWO

BUDGETS

When a person begins earning money, it is important to learn how to manage it. One of the first steps is creating a budget. John Maxwell is a leadership expert. He says, "A budget is . . . telling your money where to go, instead of wondering where it went."[3]

A budget can help teens handle their money to meet their needs and goals. Budgets help people make sure they spend

People should keep a record of how much money they are making and spending.

People may create budgets for different lengths of time. Some track money for a week or for a month.

less than they earn. People can also budget to save money for goals or emergencies. In these ways, budgets can reduce stress. They can build confidence. Budgets also help people see how they spend their money. They might notice that they could spend less money in some areas. This frees up extra money for other things.

CREATING THE BUDGET

All people have different incomes, resources, and goals. This means their budgets will be different. A teen's budget should be designed to fit their lifestyle. When setting up a budget, teens should first figure out their goals. For example, they may want to save money for a large purchase, such as a car. Having a goal makes it easier to decide how much to spend or save.

The next step is knowing how much money is coming in and out. Money coming in may include allowance, gifts, and paychecks. Then, to calculate money going out, people must figure out their expenses. These depend on people's situations. Some expenses are necessary. For example, some people must pay for rent or groceries. Teens may have necessary costs even if they live with family. These costs could include gasoline, car insurance, and clothing.

Other types of expenses are called discretionary expenses. That is when money goes toward items that someone wants but does not need. That can include eating out or going to movies. These purchases can be enjoyable. But they can also add up quickly. Shanna Skidmore is a business consultant. She explains, "A budget ensures your money goes where you *want* it to go, towards the things that actually matter to you, instead of little purchases here and there that add up."[4]

It is also important to think about saving when creating a budget. Many experts also suggest that people set aside money to

For many people, discretionary expenses may include music or other forms of entertainment.

save before they set aside money to spend. Some financial advisors recommend saving about 20 percent of income each month.

So, say a teen makes $300 a month from their part-time job. They want to make a budget. The teen's necessary expenses each month include $50 for gas and $50 for helping with the family's groceries.

Attending sporting events are common discretionary expenses.

They also want to put $60 a month in a savings account. That leaves $140 for discretionary expenses. The teen may decide to budget $50 for new clothes, $50 for eating out, and $40 for fun events.

BALANCING THE BUDGET

In some cases, budgets need adjusting. Once someone knows how much money is coming in and out, they can compare the numbers. When income is the same as expenses and savings, the budget is balanced. That is ideal. However, a person's income may be greater than their expenses. That means they will have money left over. Instead of spending more, they can save more of this money.

Sometimes, expenses are greater than income. When this happens, the person must change their spending habits. Otherwise, they will go into **debt**.

One way to balance a budget is to carefully consider each expense. Some expenses are fixed. Fixed expenses stay about the same each month. That could be the rent or phone bill. Variable expenses can change. Examples include groceries,

Giving Back

Many people like to donate to **charitable** organizations. These organizations can include churches, pet rescues, and health groups. Donating lets people support causes they care about. So, people consider these donations when building a budget. They make sure they have enough to give.

Volunteering can be a great low-cost activity for friends to do together.

clothing, eating out, or entertainment. Sometimes people find unneeded spending when they review these expenses. For example, maybe a teen notices that they spent $30 on gas station snacks. They might decide to spend less on that the next month. Or they could find cheaper activities to do with friends.

TRACKING SPENDING

After setting up a budget, it is important to track spending. For example, a teen might decide to allow $25 for eating out in their budget that month. They spend $15 on lunch with a friend. They can record that number. Then the teen knows know they have $10 left to spend on meals out for the rest of the month.

Reviewing income and expenses every month is helpful. People may find expenses they forgot to account for. Or they may decide to adjust categories in their budget for the next month.

When a person spends less than they make, it is called living within their means.

CHAPTER THREE

CREDIT AND CREDIT CARDS

Credit lets people buy things before paying for them. When people use credit, they promise to pay in the future. An organization provides the credit. They are called the lender. The lender often charges a fee, called interest. The person who uses credit must pay this fee. That is how the lender earns money.

Companies and banks often loan money through credit cards. People use credit

Credit cards contain information including the cardholder's name and card number.

CREDIT
CARD
0123 4567 8400 0000
1234
CARDHOLDER NAME

cards to make purchases. At the end of the **billing cycle**, they get a bill. People can pay back the full balance, or total owed.

People can use credit cards in person or online.

Or they may make a minimum payment. This is the smallest payment the lender will accept. The lender then adds interest to the remaining amount.

Interest rates for credit cards vary. Some new cards offer a starting interest rate of 0 percent. That means the user will not be charged a fee for borrowing money. These cards are designed to attract new users.

After a certain time, the interest rate goes up. Many credit cards have an interest rate of 20 to 30 percent per year. Over time, this can make purchases cost much more than their original price. But interest is only added if the user does not fully pay back the lender each cycle.

Many people overuse their credit cards. For example, people may spend more than their budgets allow. They may not pay their full credit card bill each month. It is also easy to lose track of how much is spent. A person's purchases and interest can grow very high. Then it is difficult for people to pay off the balance. They can go into debt.

USING CREDIT CARDS WISELY

People should stay in control of their credit card use. One way is by not using credit for more than they can afford to pay back. That way, they can pay their bills fully each month. Another option is using a secure credit card. This type requires the card holder to put down an amount of money up front. That deposit becomes the credit line for the card. Debtosh Banerjee is president of a credit building program. He says,

Debt can grow quickly, making it very difficult to pay it off.

"The key is to treat the card as a tool for building habits, not as free money."[5]

Using a credit card has advantages. Credit cards can be helpful in emergencies.

People may use credit cards to pay for unexpected expenses, such as repairs after car accidents.

For example, a person may not have enough money in the bank for a home repair or medical bill. In addition, credit card companies monitor purchases. If they notice unusual purchases, they let the cardholders know. This helps protect the owner against people stealing their cards.

For most credit cards, cardholders must be at least 18 years old. At that age, they may apply for student cards. However, they must still meet the income requirements. If they do not, they may be able to apply with a cosigner. That is a person who promises to pay the bill if the cardholder can't.

BUILDING CREDIT

Using a credit card wisely can help someone build a good credit score.

This number shows how trustworthy a borrower is. Banks and other lenders use the score to decide whether to give people loans. They may also use it to set interest rates on loans. Bruce McClary works with the National Foundation for Credit Counseling. He explains, "By using the card and making on-time payments,

Fixing Credit Scores

People can improve a low credit score. Paying balances in full each month can help raise it. If that is not possible, people can pay down the balance. Keeping up with other bills can help, too. Tom Quinn is a vice president at FICO. This company determines credit scores. Quinn explains that "you can focus on behaviors and practices that creditors look for in a borrower."

Quoted in Dawn Panadrea and Jerry Brown, "How to Increase Your Credit Score," U.S. News, *November 18, 2025. http://money.usnews.com.*

Credit scores range from 300 to 850. A good score is 690 to 850.

you are demonstrating to lenders that you're a responsible borrower."[6]

Credit scores are based on several factors. One is whether payments are made on time. How long the person has had credit matters, too. To lenders, a person with a lower credit score is riskier. It is more likely that the lender will not get their money back.

CHAPTER FOUR

BUILDING WEALTH

Saving is an important part of managing money. In addition, teens may also consider **investing**. Investing involves assets. An asset is something valuable that a person or company owns. When a person invests, they buy assets that may grow in value or earn money. For this reason, investing is often called growing or building wealth.

Teens may save cash before putting it into bank accounts.

Some people choose to invest in well-known brands and companies. They may also choose companies with similar values to theirs.

There are many ways to invest. These include buying real estate, gold, or stocks in a company. People usually hold investments for many years. It can take time for the investment's value to increase. So money made from investments is often used for long-term goals. These could include buying a house or saving for retirement.

TYPES OF INVESTMENTS

Teens have several options when investing. Stocks are one of the most common ways to build wealth. Stocks are shares of a company. Buying stocks gives someone partial ownership of the company. If the company grows, stock owners can make money. If it does not do well, investors may lose money. Stocks usually grow about 10 percent a year if they are owned for many years. This means money can grow if it stays invested for a long time.

Bonds are another type of investment. Buying a bond means lending money to someone, usually a company or the government. The investor eventually gets back the bond's value plus interest. The interest amount is fixed and does not change over time. Bonds are less risky than stocks. But they do not earn as much.

A mutual fund is a special type of investment company. It combines money from many investors. Then it invests the money in different assets, including stocks and bonds. The money is spread out across many companies instead of going to just one place. The risk of losing money is lower than when investing in a single company. Even if one company does poorly, the others help protect the money.

People can make various types of investments online.

COMPOUNDING INTEREST

Investments often grow through compound interest. Compound interest is when an investor gains interest on both the money they invested and the interest already earned. The balance gets bigger each year.

For example, a person might invest $100. They earn 5 percent interest each year. At the end of the first year, they get $5 in interest. Their new total is $105. The next year, they will earn 5 percent interest on $105. This equals $5.25. So, their new total is $110.25. Each year, the interest adds to the balance. The balance grows more and more. In 10 years, the investor has earned $62 in interest. Their $100 grew to $162.

Teens have a special opportunity due to their age. When teens invest, they may

GROWING THROUGH INTEREST

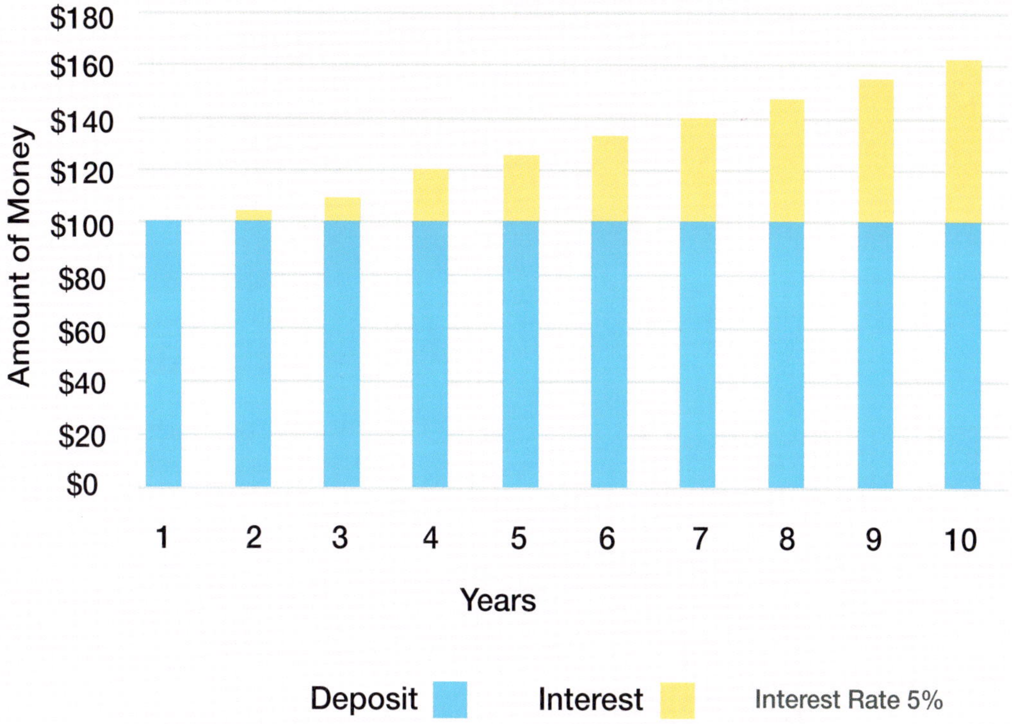

Source: "Compound Interest Calculator," NerdWallet, *n.d. www.nerdwallet.com.*

If a person invests $100 one time, the amount of interest it earns usually increases each year.

have decades of time for compound interest growth. Even small amounts can grow much larger over time. Eddie Behringer is the co-founder of Copper Banking. This is

Teens may be able to invest through education savings accounts or retirement savings accounts.

a teen financial education platform. He explains, "Time is the #1 biggest benefit to young investors. . . . There's more time for their contributions to grow."[7]

GETTING STARTED

The first step to investing is setting goals. Someone may be saving for a car, college tuition, or wealth for the future. They may want to invest money from a part-time job. To do this, teens need to open an account. A brokerage account lets people buy and sell different types of investments. Teens must be 18 years old to open their own brokerage account. If they are under 18, a parent or guardian can open a custodial account.

The next step is to decide where to invest. Teens could choose familiar companies or industries. Victor Wang works with the app Stockpile. This app helps teens learn to save and invest. Wang explains,

> *If you're thinking about investing, researching the brands you love and use every day can be a great place to start. Maybe you're a huge Nike*

The Rule of 72

People often use a shorthand called the Rule of 72 to estimate how much their investments will grow. It helps calculate how long until an investment doubles in value. The investor can divide 72 by their interest rate. The answer is the approximate number of years the investment will take to double.

Financial advisors can help people make decisions about investing.

fan. . . . You can start investing just $5 in a few of your favorite companies.[8]

It can be difficult to pick specific companies. Investors may choose safe mutual funds instead.

Investing regularly is important to building wealth. Even a small amount each month is a good start. Some people think of it as

People who learn financial literacy early make better money decisions later in life.

a formula. Regular investments plus time equals wealth. The earlier someone starts, the more time they have to save and grow money for their future.

Gaining financial literacy is important for succeeding in life. With financial literacy, people can learn how to manage the money they earn from jobs. They can budget to reduce spending and increase saving. They can build good credit from smart credit card use. And they can save money and invest to build wealth.

GLOSSARY

benefits

perks a job offers to employees, which can include insurance, paid time off, and contributions to retirement accounts

billing cycle

an amount of time before a new bill is sent

charitable

related to helping people in need

debt

money that is owed to another person or organization

deposit

to put money into a bank or credit union

income

money received for work

investing

buying stocks, bonds, or other assets that may gain value over time

service fees

extra money charged for services related to a product

SOURCE NOTES

INTRODUCTION: PAYDAY

1. Rachel Greszler, "Fewer Teens are Working, Earning Money and Job Skills," *Arizona Daily Star*, August 28, 2025. http://tuscon.com.

CHAPTER ONE: EARNING MONEY

2. Sophia Acevedo, "Best Teen Checking Accounts of 2025," *Business Insider*, April 25, 2025. www.businessinsider.com.

CHAPTER TWO: BUDGETS

3. Quoted in "Dave Rant: How to Finally Take Control of Your Money." *Ramsey Solutions*, May 1, 2023. www.ramseysolutions.com.

4. Shanna Skidmore, "Do You Really Need a Budget? A Former Financial Advisor Weighs In," *Shanna Skidmore*, June 7, 2024. www.shannaskidmore.com.

CHAPTER THREE: CREDIT AND CREDIT CARDS

5. Quoted in Rebecca Safier, "Using Your Student Credit Card Responsibly – What to Spend On and What to Avoid," *U.S. News*, September 4, 2025. http://money.usnews.com.

6. Quoted in Safier, "Using Your Student Credit Card Responsibly. "

CHAPTER FOUR: BUILDING WEALTH

7. Quoted in Liz Frazier, "Why Teenagers Should Start Investing Early … And 3 Proven Investment Tips for Any Age," *Forbes*, February 1, 2023. www.forbes.com.

8. Quoted in Kate Stalter, "Investing for Teens: How to Invest Money as a Teenager," *U.S. News*, June 16, 2025. http://money.usnews.com.

FOR FURTHER RESEARCH

BOOKS

Ferne Bowe. *Money Skills for Teens*. Bemberton, 2023.

Jenny Crooks-Johnson, *Managing Income*. BrightPoint Press, 2027.

Kris Erickson Rowley, *Quick Guide to Saving and Investing*. BrightPoint Press, 2025.

INTERNET SOURCES

Emmanuel Modu, "How To Invest Under Age 18," *TeenVestor*, January 3, 2026. www.teenvestor.com.

Cyrus Vanover, "Teen Budgeting Guide: 6 Steps to Healthy Financial Habits," *Citizens Bank*, n.d. www.citizensbank.com.

"What Is Compounding and Compound Interest? A Simple Explanation for Kids, Teens & Beginners," *Easy Peasy Finance*, n.d. www.easypeasyfinance.com.

WEBSITES

Hands on Banking

https://youth.handsonbanking.org

This free financial education site helps people learn money management skills through lessons, activities, and courses.

Federal Trade Commission

http://consumer.gov

This website includes clear, simple information about many money topics, including debt, budgeting, and loans.

Practical Money Skills

www.practicalmoneyskills.com

This site provides games, tools, and resources to help people build financial skills.

INDEX

IMAGE CREDITS

Cover: © Andrii Lemelianenko/Shutterstock Images
5: © Supavadee Butradee/Shutterstock Images
7: © Mike_shots/Shutterstock Images
8: © Johnstocker Production/Shutterstock Images
11: © Lopolo/Shutterstock Images
12: © metamorworks/Shutterstock Images
15: © Quality Stock Arts/Shutterstock Images
17: © Pranithan Chorruangsak/Shutterstock Images
18: © TStudious/Shutterstock Images
21: © Jim Bethel/Shutterstock Images
23: © Rodica Vasiliev/Shutterstock Images
24: © MarinelaM/Shutterstock Images
27: © Zamrznuti Tonovi/Shutterstock Images
28: © Gorodenkoff/Shutterstock Images
31: © Baza Production/Shutterstock Images
33: © CandyRetriever/Shutterstock Images
35: © New Africa/Shutterstock Images
36: © Pixel-Shot/Shutterstock Images
39: © Shurkin_Son/Shutterstock Images
40: © anek.soowannaphoom/Shutterstock Images
43: © Prostock-Studio/Shutterstock Images
45: © LightField Studios/Shutterstock Images
46: © Jan von Uxkull-Gyllenband/Shutterstock Images
49: © Shyntartanya/Shutterstock Images
51: Red Line Editorial
52: © Ground Picture/Shutterstock Images
55: © PeopleImages/Shutterstock Images
56: © Pixel-Shot/Shutterstock Images

ABOUT THE AUTHOR

Samantha S. Bell lives in the foothills of the Blue Ridge Mountains with her family and lots of cats. She is the author of more than 200 nonfiction books for students. She knows the power of budgeting, saving, and planning ahead!